Trucks!

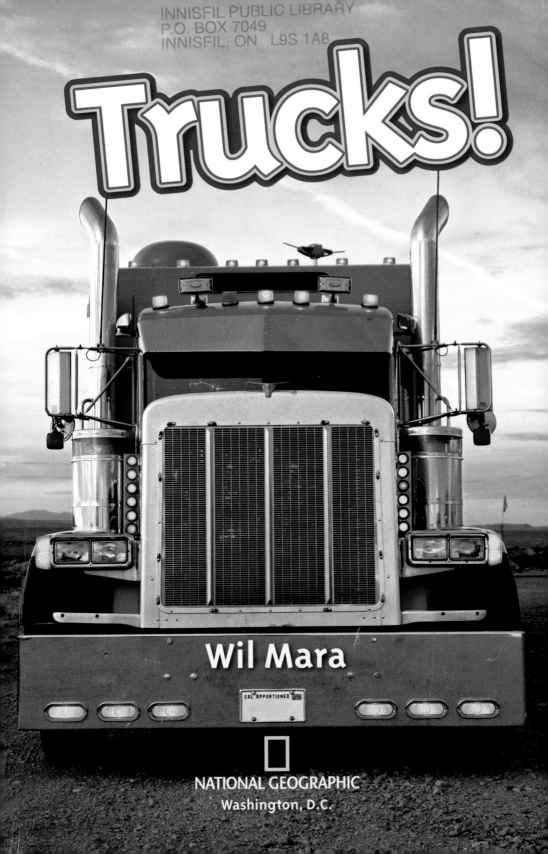

Wil Mara

NATIONAL GEOGRAPHIC
Washington, D.C.

For Andy and Scott, who know more
about trucks than I ever will. — W.M.

Text copyright © 2009 National Geographic Society

Published by the National Geographic Society, Washington, D.C. 20036. All rights reserved.
Reproduction in whole or in part without written permission of the publisher is strictly prohibited.

Library of Congress Cataloging-in-Publication Data
Mara, Wil.
Trucks / Wil Mara.
p. cm.
ISBN 978-1-4263-0526-9 (paperback : alk. paper) -- ISBN 978-1-4263-0527-6 (library binding : alk. paper)
1. Trucks--Juvenile literature. I. Title.
TL230.15.M366 2009
629.225--dc22
2009021037

Printed in the United States of America

All photos of "Slick" © Mark Thiessen/NationalGeographicStock.com; Cover: © Walter Hodges/ Photographer's Choice/
Getty Images; 1: © Christopher Thomas/ Photographer's Choice/ Getty Images; 2: © Code Red/ Getty Images; 5: © Brian
Sullivan; 6-7, 32 (top, left): © Lester Lefkowitz/ Stone/ Getty Images; 8-9: © Alain Le Bot/ Photolibrary; 10: © AP Photo/ Pat
Sullivan; 12-13: © Guy Crittenden/ Photographer's Choice RF/ Getty Images; 14-15: © Donald R. Swartz/ Shutterstock; 16-17:
© Daniel Valla FRPS/ Alamy; 17 (right inset), 32 (bottom, left): © age footstock/ SuperStock; 18-19: © Scott Olson/ Getty
Images; 20-21: © Ian Dagnall/ Alamy; 22-23: © Stuart Walker/ Alamy; 24-25: © Joe Baraban/ Transtock/ JupiterImages;
26-27: © Fernando Rodrigues/ Shutterstock; 28-29, 32 (bottom, right): © Robert Kerian/ Transtock/ Alamy; 30: © Richard
Leeney/ Dorling Kindersley/ DK Images; 32 (top, right): © Dorling Kindersley/ Getty Images

Table of Contents

Meet Slick

Hi, I'm Slick.
Do you like trucks?
I sure do. Big or small,
I like them ALL!

Dump Truck

A dump truck carries sand, rocks, and dirt. The back of the truck is like a big box.

hydraulic cylinders

Two hydraulic cylinders push the box up and **Whoosh!** the load spills out.

Say *Hi-draw-lik sil-en-ders.*

TRUCK TALK

Hydraulic Cylinders: Tubes filled with oil

Tow Truck

Oh, no. This car needs a ride. A tow truck pushes its flat bed to the street. Chains hook to the axle of the car and pull it onto the bed. They hold it tight for a ride to the shop.

Garbage Truck

hydraulic cylinder

Our landfills provide over 12,000 acres of wildlife habitat.

Garbage trucks have major mojo! This front loader lifts a big trash bin. Up and over goes the garbage. It is tipped in, crunched back, smushed and pushed.

Check out these hydraulics!

209073

MACK

Cement Mixer

The best part of a cement mixer is the drum. If it's rolling, the truck has new cement inside. The drum cannot stop rolling. If it does, the cement will harden in the drum.

Fire Truck

There are all kinds of fire trucks.
This one is a pump truck. It
pumps water. It has hoses and
a water cannon.

A pump truck hooks up to a hydrant to get water.

water cannon

www.kearnyusa.com

Tanker Truck

A tanker truck carries fluid, like milk. There is a hatch on top of the tank, where the tank is filled.

TRUCK TALK

Hatch: The door that covers a small opening.

first milk

Wincanton

hatch

hatch

first milk

Car Transport

How cool is this?

It's a car transport.

upper deck

It carries new cars on its trailer. The trailer has upper decks and a lower deck. The upper decks are lifted by hydraulics.

Check it out! Hydraulics!

lower deck

An armored truck has a bulletproof shell. Even the windows and tires are bulletproof.

Heavy Hauler

Some trucks have big jobs.

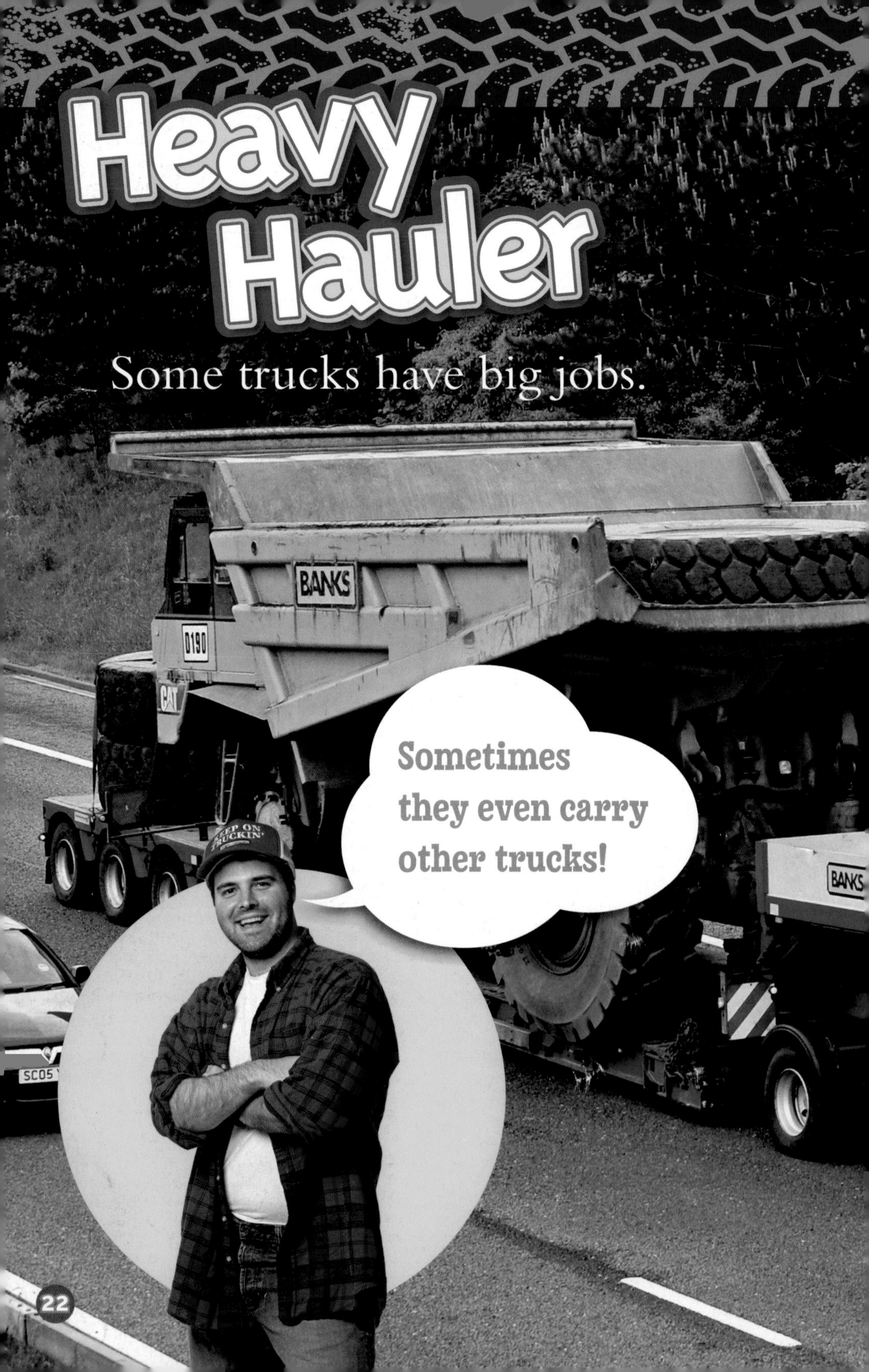

A heavy hauler carries big things, like houses and airplanes. It needs a lot of wheels. These trucks are also called 18-wheelers.

Liebherr T282

This is one of the biggest trucks in the world. It's a dump truck. The driver has to climb a ladder just to get into the seat! It also has video cameras so the driver can see on all sides. It can carry more than 50 schoolbuses. This truck costs 3 million dollars!

Slick's Big Rig

Here is my rig.
It is a tractor trailer.
The tractor part is
the front. It pulls
the trailer.

Slick's Office

speedometer

TRUCK TALK

Dashboard: *Where all the controls for the truck are found*

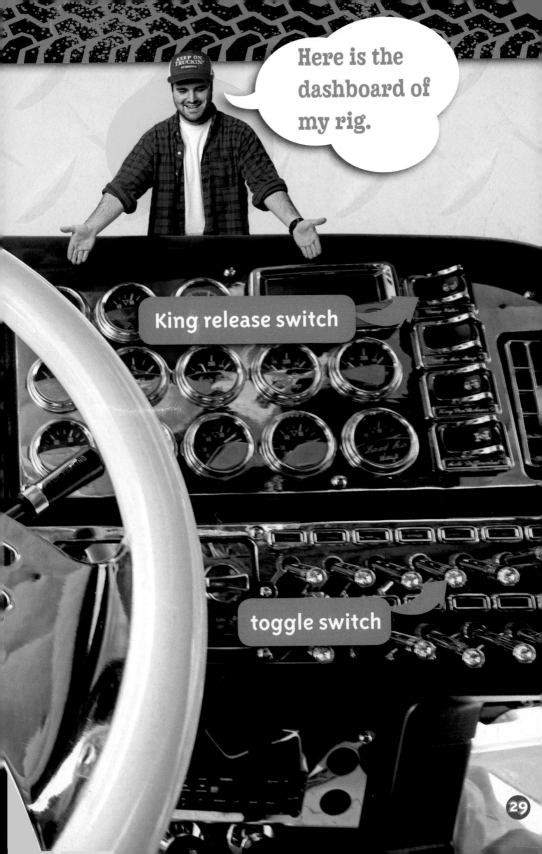

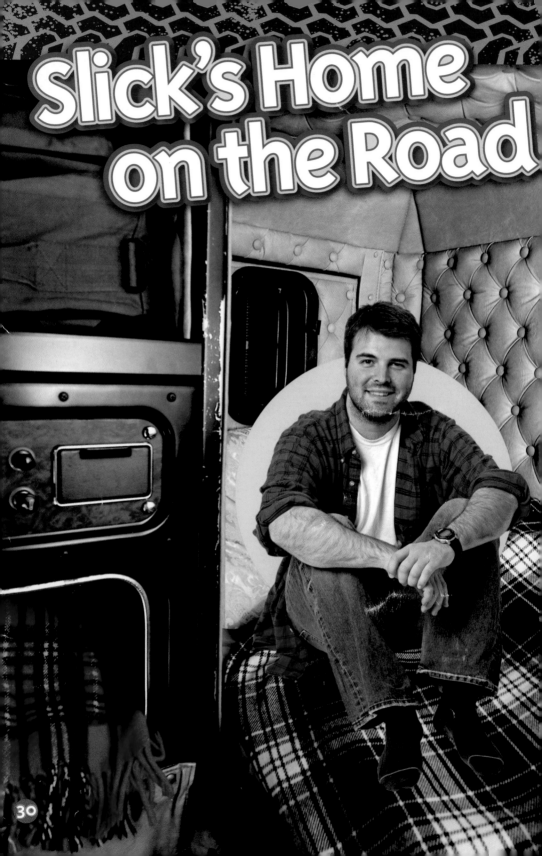

Slick's Home on the Road

I can pull off the road and sleep in my cab. This is my home away from home. I love my truck!

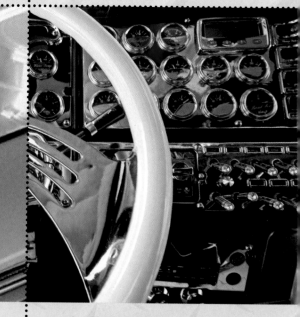

HYDRAULIC CYLINDERS
Tubes filled with oil

AXEL
The rod between two wheels

HATCH
The door that covers
a small opening

DASHBOARD
Where all the controls for the
truck are found